Venezuelan mountain savannas are very frequent at the altitudinal level of mountain forests. Their great extension certainly results from the activities of Man. After the initial destruction of the forest these savannas have been maintained thanks to agricultural activities or to occasional or periodic fires (not necessarily annual).

A predominant herbaceous cover gives its physiognomy to mountain savannas. In this sense they have many similarities with the Llanos, specially with those not periodically flooded, with the common presence of the genera *Byrsonima, Trachypogon, Paspalum, Axonopus, Desmodium...* But not all species are present in both and the same species may have different frequencies in mountain savannas and in the Llanos.

In mountain savannas we can observe *Schoenocaulon officinale* (LILIACEAE), *Bletia* (ORCHIDACEAE), *Sinningia incarnata* (GESNERIACEAE), *Hippeastrum solandrifolium* (AMARYLLIDACEAE), *Stevia* and *Chaptalia* (ASTERACEAE) and the fern *Pteridium aquilinum*, but there are also some differences between the savannas of different mountain ranges.

We can find in mountain savannas many geophytes. They have underground organs that allow them to survive the dry season and to fire (bulbs, tubers, rhizomes).

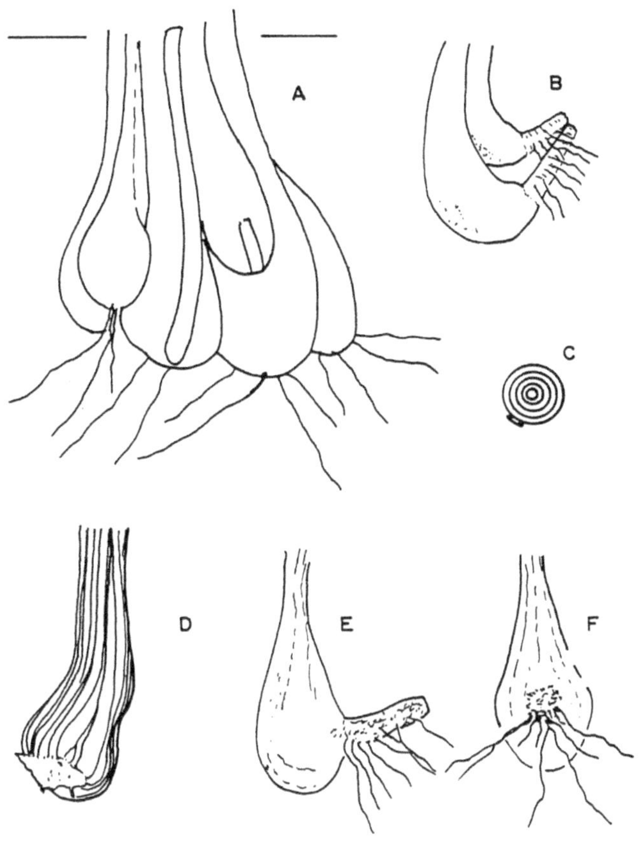

A
B
C
D
E
F

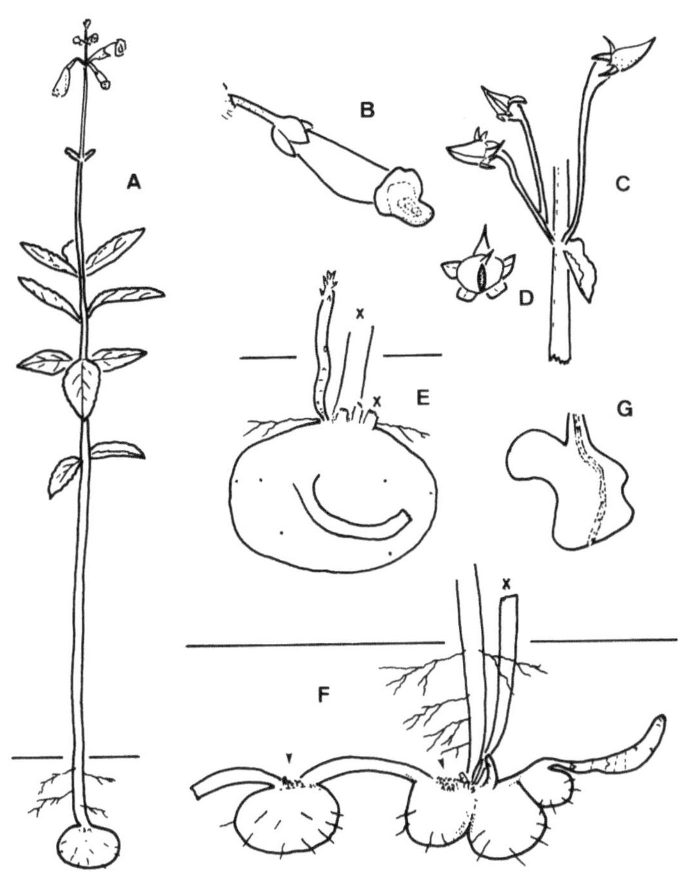

A
B
C
D
E
x
x
G
F
x

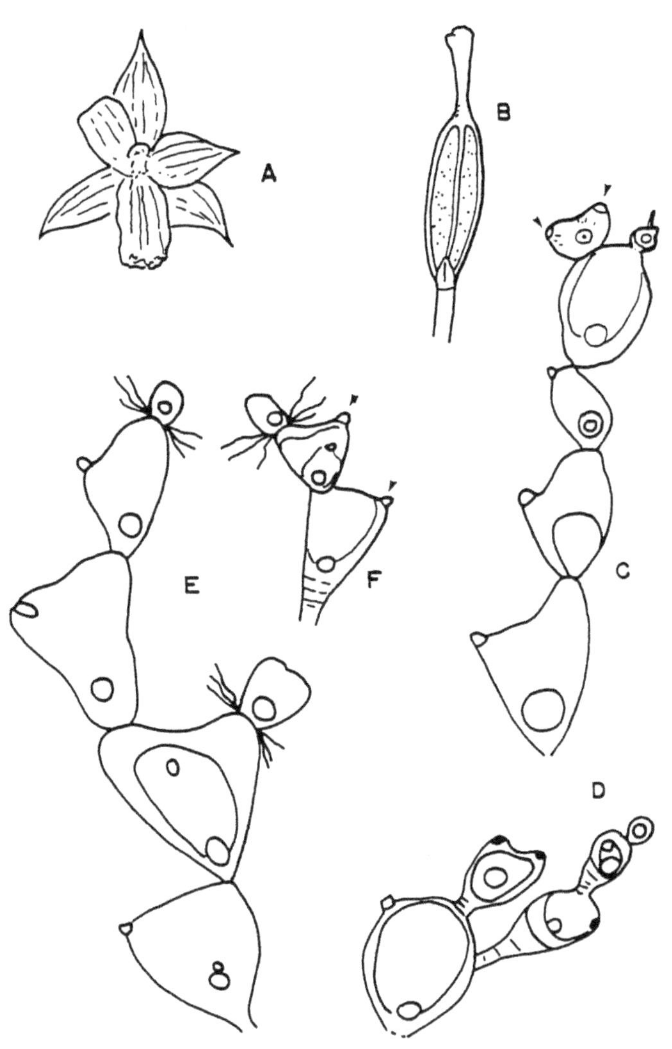